CYCLING KING ALFRED'S WAY

CYCLING KING ALFRED'S WAY

A PIECE OF CAKE?

Julia Goodfellow-Smith

Cycling King Alfred's Way
Cycling King Alfred's Way

Published by Julia Goodfellow-Smith
First published in 2022

ISBN – paperback: 978-0-86319-483-2
ISBN – e-book: 978-0-86319-484-9
ISBN – audiobook: 978-0-86319-485-6

Cycling King Alfred's Way is dedicated to Ali and Bob,
for decades of friendship.

Table of Contents

Foreword

Cycling King Alfred's Way represents so many things for different people. For some, it's a way to engage all their senses as they ride through the beautiful countryside between some of the most iconic sites in the UK. For experienced cyclists, it's a chance to ride 350km along a carefully curated route that brings out the best of Salisbury Plain, the Ridgeway, the Surrey Hills and the South Downs.

For non-cyclist Julia Goodfellow-Smith, it was a perfect choice for her latest bucket list challenge. This wonderfully inspiring story follows her personal journey through spin class training and a literal crash course in off-road riding with her King Alfred's Way partner and mountain bike mentor, Ali. But it's more than just a look back at her adventure. It's also an education in every part of preparing for this epic ride, written in a way anyone can understand and everyone will enjoy.

Guy Kesteven
Author of the Cycling UK King Alfred's Way guidebook and creator of www.pedallingpast.com

A Spin Through Time

King Alfred's Way. The name is beguiling in itself, but it doesn't tell the whole story. The route does not just pass Alfred The Great's birthplace (Wantage) and final resting place (Winchester), but sites from throughout England's history. As you cycle King Alfred's Way, you skirt the mystical stones of Stonehenge and Avebury, numerous Iron Age hill forts and two cathedral cities. You cross sparkling chalk streams flanked by flint and thatch cottages. You mount the hulking mass of Salisbury Plain and pick your way along the northern edge of the Berkshire Downs. You descend the gentle Thames Valley and crunch through the gravelly woodlands of Berkshire before sinking onto the sandy soils of the Surrey Hills. And finally, you climb onto the unyielding chalk of the South Downs with spectacular views over the English Channel.

As soon as I heard about King Alfred's Way, I was hooked.

'Look, Ali. Have you seen this? It's a new cycling route. It's 200 miles long and mainly off-road. Shall we ride it together?'

'OK, let's do it!'

This book tells our tale of tackling King Alfred's Way, including what I learnt while training and during the ride itself. If you are an experienced cycle tourer, you will gain an insight into the route. If you are a novice like me, it will help you prepare for any multi-day cycling adventure you are considering.

The first section chronicles my journey from walking fit to cycling fit in six weeks, followed by my experience of the ride itself. It's an adventure story that is also bursting with useful information for anyone planning a cycle trip.

The second section will help you organise your own trip. It is structured around the process detailed in *Live Your Bucket List* — igniting your dream, planning, overcoming obstacles, implementing your plan and the final step of celebrating and reflecting on your journey.

This is followed by a bonus chapter: Ali's Response.

Next time I go cycle touring, I'll do things differently. I'll learn from my mistakes and magnify my successes. By reading this book, you can do the same, and your trip will be better for it.

Read on to hear more about my journey from cycling ugly duckling to spinning swan. Keep your eyes peeled and a highlighter ready for the juicy bits of insight that will help you with your preparations...

My journey

Excitement Mounts

Standing at their perfectly polished kitchen counter, the smell of lunch still lingering in the air, I feel the familiar sensation of butterflies in my stomach — something that has been missing until now.

Alison and I have just set a date for cycling King Alfred's Way. We have been talking about it for months. Now we've set the date, the trip has moved from possibility to probability.

I am active but rarely ride a bike. I am not even remotely cycle-fit. Alison, on the other hand, is a keen mountain biker. She is incredibly fit and cycles a lot. This is going to be more of a challenge for me than for her. I don't even have a functioning bike.

Luckily, Alison and her partner, Bob, have spare bikes and have offered to lend me one. As the day progresses, I slowly realise that when Bob says, 'I'll get a bike ready for you as soon as I can,' what he means is, 'I'm going to build you a bike from scratch!'

'I was browsing for parts and came across two frames that were going cheap as well as the one I needed for my dream bike, so I bought all three. Now I've got all the parts I need, I'm building my dream bike. I'll do yours next.'

'I'll lend you a lightweight cycling waterproof and a pair of mountain-biking shoes,' Ali added. 'They stick well to the pedals. You'll need some padded shorts and a rucksack with a hydration bladder. Now, how about timings? I think we should plan to do it in four days. Do you agree?'

My eyes widened in horror. On roads, 54 miles a day would be challenging but achievable, but off-road? I think it is too ambitious. Luckily, Bob agrees with me.

'When we go mountain biking, we only cover about six miles an hour. If you maintain that speed, you would have to cycle for nine hours a day. You could both manage that, but you would just be focusing on getting to the end each day... and you wouldn't have time to stop for tea and cake.'

Those are the winning words — it is settled. We will plan to complete the route in five days, ending on a Friday so that we can take six if we need to.

'I'll take the week off work, so I'm around if you need any technical support,' Bob adds. What a star!

I borrow Bob's old bike and we set off through the trees onto the heath. I am just beginning to think that I can do this when a hill bites back. The track ahead leads steeply up into the trees. Alison is in front, powering up the slope. I am pedalling hard in a very low gear, pulling on the handlebars to help me push down better on the pedals, when I lose traction and momentum. I'm doing a wheelie, and it's enough to stop me in my tracks.

Pride Comes Before a Fall

'We're almost back now.'

'Please don't say that!'

These words are dangerous for me. My brain doesn't hear the 'almost' part and simply decides it is time to stop. If I think or hear these words, the final part of my journey becomes a mental and physical battle. It's even worse when it isn't true and just said as 'encouragement'.

We have been out cycling for 90 minutes so far; longer than I have been in the saddle for years. It is August and I am starting to train in earnest.

We set off into the pine woods and heathland in glorious summer sunshine, although the ground is damp and muddy in places from earlier rain. This bike does not have mudguards, so a sticky brown stripe is growing up my back. But it's not just the back wheel that is generating spray. I hope it's just mud that is coating my teeth and tongue. My mouth feels gritty and tastes earthy.

We pedal up sandy slopes, over fallen trees, through muddy puddles and along narrow, winding paths. I am impressed with how well the wide mountain bike tyres manage both the terrain and my lack of skill. On a couple of occasions, I misaim and cycle over tree stumps, and the bike just takes them in its stride.

As I grind my way up a small but steep slope with pebbles crunching beneath me, my back wheel spins and then the front wheel lifts off the ground. I had forgotten to keep my weight distributed — and to pull backwards on the handlebars, not upwards.

Moments later, the heavens open, drenching us both. The world disappears behind the thick mist that instantly forms on my glasses. I can't tell which bits of the path are soft pine needles and which are exposed tree roots, ready to snag my tyres and send me flying. It is a perfect excuse to stop for a moment, catch my breath and appreciate the smells released by the summer rain.

Alison is a much better cyclist than me and is pushing me today. This is only our second ride out together this summer, and I am already improving. I am feeling rather proud of my performance.

I remember the hill from our last ride. That time, Ali had warned me about it, but I made it to the top without too much trouble. At that time, I was fresh. This time, I have already been cycling for an hour. Alison is in front of me, grinding slowly up the slope. I catch her up and then stall.

An unhelpful notion creeps into my mind: 'You can always get off and push if you need to.' Almost as soon as it appears, I just can't cycle any further. With one short thought, I had talked myself out of reaching the top.

'What went wrong?'

'I caught you up and couldn't overtake.'

'OK, let's try again. You first this time.'

I force out unhelpful thoughts with positive ones: 'You've got this, Julia.' And, 'You've done this before; you can do it again.'

It works — I make it all the way to the top while still pedalling this time. There is a price to pay, though. When Alison catches up with me, I am still leaning against a tree, gasping for breath.

She suggests that we should do the same climb again.

'No!'

A few miles of easy riding later and she utters those words, 'We're almost back now.' I try to overwrite them in my brain. 'Keep going, Julia, you've got this!'

As we make the final turn off the main path towards the end of our ride, I recognise it.

'We really are almost back now!'

I should know better. Once again, my brain switches off. The path narrows. Rhododendrons are crowding in. The branches are as contorted as the path itself, and the twigs scratch my skin. Like something from the Forbidden Forest, a branch shoots out and grabs my front wheel. I try to swerve, but it's too late. The front of my bike stops abruptly. The back doesn't, and nor do I.

Lying underneath the bike and the rhododendron bush, I can feel the heat rising up my ears. I have not fallen off a bike for years. And now I've done it in front of my friend Ali, who will never let me forget it. Luckily, nothing hurts except my pride. A laugh bubbles up to the surface, erupting into the silence. It is shortly joined by hers.

Now, I am not quite as pleased with my performance. I am pleased that I have started training for cycling King Alfred's Way, though — I obviously need the practice!

Freaked Out

After the ride, I relax under a hot shower and think about how some people pay good money to be caked in mud like this. It is streaming off me and snaking along the length of the bath to the drain.

'Why isn't this spot of mud washing off?' I wonder, rubbing it. My brain races. Maybe it's not mud. Maybe it's a tick. I don't wear my glasses in the shower, so the blob is a bit fuzzy, but are they legs I can see against my own?

'Perhaps it will let go if I make it hot.' Ever optimistic, I turn around and run the shower directly over my leg. The blob stays in place. I remember that you shouldn't stress a tick. If you do, they can regurgitate their stomach contents into your body. The thought of that makes me feel queasy.

'Breathe, Julia!'

I quickly turn the water off and towel down, careful to avoid that part of my leg. I put my glasses on for a clearer look. It is definitely a tick. I can see its body and legs. I can also see that its head is burrowed into my skin. My heart palpitates and my mind spins. I have to get it out. Now!

For a moment, I am not sure that I can find the courage to remove the tick myself. I imagine asking Alison to remove it for me and realise how embarrassed I would be. There is nothing for it — I will have to do it.

In my calmest possible voice: 'Alison, do you have a tick-removal tool, please?'

To my relief, she finds one almost immediately. I take a few deep breaths as I fit the tick's body into the V of the tool, twist gently and pull. It is out. Thank goodness for that!

In his usual no-nonsense way, Bob dispatches the wriggling bug. 'It's good that it was moving. That means you got the whole thing out. Well done!'

My mind turns to the risk of getting Lyme disease. This seems to be becoming more prevalent in the UK and can make you very unwell. I removed the tick quickly, so the chances of becoming ill are slim. But I will still keep an eye out for the tell-tale symptoms or bull's eye rings appearing on my leg.

This episode has given me a great incentive not to fall again, if only to avoid the ticks. But is it enough to overcome my lack of off-road experience? Only time will tell.

The Ride to Nowhere

During my first week of training, neither the mountain bike nor my ancient hybrid bike is ready to ride, so I book myself into a couple of spinning classes. Alison swears by these to improve her cycling fitness.

I peer around the door. A dozen or so bikes are lined up in rows of semi-circles around what is presumably the instructor's bike. I choose an empty one and apprehensively walk towards it. Everyone else is effortlessly cycling the pedals around, waiting for the class to start.

I look at the bike. There are pegs and levers all over the place. I can probably work out what height to set the seat, but have no idea how to set up the rest of the bike. How far forwards should the seat be? How high should the handlebars be? And how far forwards or backwards should they be? How do I adjust the straps for my feet?

I look around, find a friendly looking face and ask how to set it up. I join the others in their rhythmic movement, feet spinning but going nowhere.

The instructor appears and saunters towards his bike. He starts the music. I want to be able to walk home after the class, so I take it easy. Too easy. The only things that hurt that evening are one of my knees and my feet — barefoot shoes and knobbly pedals are not a good combination.

When I arrive for the next lesson, a different instructor tells me how to set up the bike. The class is better because I am working harder, but my knee and feet are even more painful.

This is not much fun, but I need to get cycle-fit fast, so I continue to go a couple of times a week.

Next time I see him, Bob teaches me how to set up the bike properly so that my knee is not under as much pressure and Alison lends me a pair of cycling shoes. The classes become more bearable, but I still have no idea why anyone would choose to do this. Being subjected to ceaseless thumping music in a confined space is my idea of torture. Why do it to yourself, when you could be out in the fresh air, riding a real bike? I am just going to have to trust Alison on the value of this one.

On the day of my final class, I am in a foul mood. The last thing that I want to do is go spinning. I set off reluctantly, walking from home with my head down, muttering to myself about how unfair life is. I am not looking forward to it.

By this point, I know the routine when I arrive. I wipe the bike over with anti-viral spray and blue roll. I set it up to fit me. I say a cursory 'hello' to the regulars who now recognise me.

When the music starts, I am still in a grump. It is a new instructor, nicknamed 'the Queen of Hover'. She has us up on our feet, pedalling fast, hovering just above the saddle, for a large part of the class.

What a waste of time, I think. This isn't a movement you do on a real bike.

I am right, but am glad of the practice later as I careen down long slopes on King Alfred's Way, hovering over the dropped seat. Although the instructor is young, she has chosen a 1980s playlist that takes me back to my teenage years. By about halfway through the class, my head is up and I am mentally singing along. What fun this is! What a difference a bit of exercise and some great music can make!

Pushing Uphill

As my training progresses, my body is getting used to sitting on a bike, and my legs are getting used to hauling me around. My speed is steadily increasing. On the bigger, steeper hills, I still have to get off and push, but I have already noticed my confidence and ability improving, uphill and down.

It is time to train off-road.

Bob has lent me his old but still very good mountain bike. He took the front wheel off to fit it in the boot of my car and showed me how to reattach it. That gives me one more thing to worry about — will I be able to reattach it correctly, or will it fall off while I'm cycling? If it does, what will happen? Will the wheel disappear over the side of the hill, never to be seen again? Will I?

This morning, I find myself faffing around — a definite sign of nervousness. The Malvern Hills are an unforgiving place for a beginner to train, and I am not sure that I am up to it.

I go to the shops to buy a hydration bladder and handlebar bag. I play around with the contents of my first aid kit. I pack and repack the rucksack I am using. I argue that I need to do all these things, but in reality, I know that it is displacement activity — keeping myself busy to avoid doing what I know needs to be done.

Eventually, I run out of excuses. I load everything into the car and drive up onto the hills. Replacing the front wheel seems simple enough, although I am not absolutely confident that the spindle will remain in place. I cautiously set off up the track.

Within only a couple of minutes, I am gasping for breath. I just cannot get the amount of oxygen I need into my body. It is time to stop and admire the view. I am an expert at using transferrable skills — it's an age-old tactic that every hillwalker knows well!

Having regained a degree of composure, I continue up the gentle slope and along to Green Valley, where the track steepens. I fight against gravity for only a few seconds before succumbing to the inevitable. I dismount and push. Even pushing a bike up such a steep and stony slope is hard work, so I am relieved to reach the top.

The next section of path is easier — an old carriage track that runs along a contour of the hills. A smile plays on my face as I wind my way along this relatively flat section, admiring the view over the Severn Valley. The Cotswolds and Bredon Hill rise in the distance, linked by a patchwork of villages and fields to Great Malvern below me. The river extends along the length of the valley, but is not visible today. The thick tree cover lower down the hills has petered out into bracken and grass, opening up the vista. A colourful jay grabs my attention as it swoops across the bracken and lands in one of the trees I have just passed. I have seen this view hundreds of times, but it never fails to delight.

Before heading down the far side of the hills, I wait for some walkers and mountain bikers to pass. One of the mountain bikers does a double-take, looks admiringly at the bike I am riding and comments on how good it is. I feel like a total fraud. The bike makes me look like an expert when, in reality, I am a complete novice.

I slowly make my way downhill, giving the brakes more exercise than Bob has probably ever applied to them. To climb back over the hills to finish my ride, I have to dismount and push three times, despite the low gears. This might be a good route for building off-road skills, but it is not good for building confidence in my hill climbing ability.

The final descent is hellish. The path is narrow with steep switchbacks that are way beyond my capability, so I spend more time off the bike as I negotiate the tight bends. To add to the challenge, the switchback path is particularly popular with walkers. It is a very slow descent.

My heart is pounding and my legs are wobbling like blancmange as I arrive at the car. I am glad to be back in one piece, and with the front wheel of the bike still attached. I haven't had to peel myself off the gravel path or climb down into a quarry to rescue the wheel!

I set out the next day hoping that I would be more confident on the gravelly tracks and steep slopes. I start in a similar vein, taking a break almost immediately. That view is rather wonderful. Who wouldn't stop to admire it?

Onwards and upwards, I cycle... and push. I am more confident today, braking less on the downhill stretches, but am I more able? Not yet. Unless, of course, you count the ability to push a bike uphill. I am getting pretty good at that. This is, of course, why I am training.

I laugh when I see that Strava has awarded me 'Local Legend on rocky switchback descent'. It is a clever app, but not clever enough to tell that I walked the bike around every switchback.

I know that I won't be able to cover long distances on the hills, and I want to get used to sitting on a bike for extended periods. So, it is time to find a longer, flatter route to build endurance. Where can I go?

Towpath Trouble

After pondering this for a while, the perfect route for cycling distances off-road comes to mind — the local canal towpath. I spin up to the station and hop on a train. It is an Intercity train with a special holding area for bikes. My bike is a beast and doesn't fit. The only option is to leave it with the wheel sticking out into the corridor. Luckily, the conductor is relaxed, and the train is nearly empty.

The towpath is crowded. I cycle slowly, dodging lovers walking hand-in-hand, elderly people weaving from one side of the path to the other, parents with pushchairs and people with dogs. Dogs! They have no idea what to do when a bike is approaching. More often than not, they stand sideways, blocking as much of the path as possible. A few times, I have to dismount and push my way past.

As usual, the crowds dissipate not far from the city centre and the cycling starts to flow. The surface of the path is varied, and not all easy-going. As I bounce over a section of exposed tree roots, I am exceptionally grateful that this bike has suspension.

There are 59 locks along this section of the canal, so plenty of uphill bits to challenge my legs. Often, the locks challenge my steering too, with a narrow ramp to aim for between steps.

Not long into the ride, pain shoots up my arms. My hands are already bruised, and my neck gradually stiffens. My toes feel like they are pushing against red-hot coals. Cue worry — again. How would I manage cycling for hour after hour, day after day, when I hurt so much after cycling for just a couple of hours? I don't remember cycling ever being this uncomfortable before. What am I doing wrong?

I give myself a good talking-to. For now, I just need to suck it up and keep the pedals turning to get my hours in and make it home. I distract myself by admiring the view. The swans here have had a good year. A lot of their cygnets have survived and are now the same size as their parents, although not yet pearly white. Mostly, they simply swim serenely along the canal, ignoring me. On a couple of occasions, I come across a family group on the towpath. When I cycle slowly around them, they hiss in consternation. One group completely fills the path and doesn't move an inch as I approach. I don't want to have a fight with a flock of swans, so I dismount and carefully pick my way between them.

The cycle back to Worcester starts fast and fun. Having ridden up 59 locks to get to where I was, I have 59 locks to cycle back down. This is something I love about cycling that you just don't get when walking — the joy of relaxing as you freewheel down the hills.

And then disaster strikes. Climbing a short uphill section to summit a tunnel, I hear a grinding noise and lose all power. I look down. The chain is dangling off the sprockets, broken. Bob has ridden this bike in all sorts of crazy conditions. I thought that it was unbreakable, but I have proved that it is not.

I crouch down to start a fingertip search of the gravel path. I am not hopeful that I will find the missing link that is smaller than the gravel and about the same colour.

To my astonishment, after just a few seconds, I find it. I don't know what to do with it, so I pop it into my pocket and then check how far I am from the train station. It will take me 3-4 hours to walk back. That's a long walk pushing a bike. Surely there's another solution?

I look up and spot two people cycling towards me. Maybe they know how to fix a chain. They have a chain repair kit with them, but no spare links of the right size. The piece I have already found is only half of what has fallen off. This time, three of us drop down to our hands and knees and hunt for the other half.

'Found it!'

What good luck! Not only have I found the missing part, but it is the connecting link that has come apart, so it is fairly easy to put back on. My towpath angels show me how to re-fit the chain link, oil my chain and set me back on my way. Although they have been so helpful, as I set off, I hope that the fix will last and I won't see them again.

Back home, I reflect on what I have learnt. I have remembered that you can break the chain by changing gear when it is under pressure. I knew this as a child but had forgotten. It is easy enough to reduce the tension at the right time, and comes back to me naturally — just like riding a bike!

I have also learnt that it's a good idea to carry a spare chain link in your tool kit.

That evening, I ask Alison about the pain in my wrists, arms and neck.

'The same thing happened to me when I started cycling. You need to relax. Stop holding onto the handlebars so tightly, and don't slump forwards.'

Unfortunately, there is nothing she can suggest to relieve my saddle-soreness. I will just have to toughen up.

On my next towpath trip, I employ all of Alison's advice and it works like a treat. I find myself smiling as I cycle along, feeling pleased that things are coming together.

A woman ahead of me steps to one side and encourages the small girl holding her hand to do the same. The little girl points up at me, eyes wide. 'Mummy, it's a *lady*!' A little while later, two lads see me coming and step out of my way. One of them looks to the other also with his eyes wide and exclaims, '*Her* bike's better than *mine*!'

What a terrible shame that young girls are surprised to see someone female on a mountain bike and that other cyclists are surprised that a woman is riding such a good bike. I'm so pleased that they have seen me — and hopefully adjusted their preconceptions about what girls and women can do with their lives.

Whether this woman will be able to cycle the whole of King Alfred's Way is still up for debate, but the time has come to find out.

King Alfred's Way: Winchester to Market Lavington

I wake with butterflies flitting around in my stomach. Today is the day that I will find out whether my training has worked. Today is the day that the real adventure starts.

While we are eating breakfast, Bob delves into his toolbox and sorts out some essentials for us. With the tools, our packs weigh 4.5kg each, including our clothes for three days. Not bad!

As I fill my hydration bladder, the nerves I have felt since waking turn into excitement. My emotions flip-flop between the two all morning.

We fix the bikes onto the roof of the car and set off towards Winchester. We find a parking space and public toilets right next to the bronze statue of King Alfred. The larger-than-life Alfred stands proudly on a high stone mount, holding his sword aloft and shield by his side, seemingly laying claim to the city. The next time I see this statue, I'll be finishing my ride as it marks the end of the circuitous route.

It is almost lunchtime. We have about 8 hours of daylight left and at least 7 hours of cycling before we arrive at our overnight stop. We don't have lamps with us, so we are cutting things fine, but our bikes are back on the ground and Bob is ready to see us off.

After the obligatory photo by the statue, we are under way!

We push our bikes along the pedestrian street to Westgate, one of the last remnants of the city's fortified defences. We roll our bikes under the medieval stone archway and officially begin our adventure.

We start with a bit of a wiggle through Winchester, but it is not long before we are on quiet lanes and into the countryside.

They are generally surfaced, so I don't have to concentrate on the riding too much. We pass through picture-postcard English villages. We see black and white houses with thatched roofs, flint houses and pretty village churches. We cross sparkling clear chalk streams, with vivid green plants waving in the flow, fish treading water and swans gliding serenely above it all. The breeze is rustling leaves in the trees above us. I think I might have found heaven!

Alison is not so keen. She loves the challenge of cycling across difficult terrain, so is finding these sections of road-riding rather boring. And boy, does she let me know it!

'What a slog!'

'80% off-road, my foot!'

'Are we nearly there yet?' OK, so I made that last one up, but you get the gist.

We stop for a quick cuppa at the Tally Ho! in Broughton, but we don't have time to relax if we want to arrive in daylight.

The guidebook warns of a tricky climb out of the village. It is a steep off-road section with a damp, rooty surface. Alison powers ahead, full of beans and delighting in a bit of off-road cycling. I try to emulate her energy, but do not make it to the top in one. I am proud of myself for not pushing, though - I simply stop partway up, catch my breath and then set off again. Alison has taught me to drop my seat and set off diagonally if I do have to stop on a hill, so at least I no longer have to push the bike if I do grind to a halt.

From the top, the route follows a Roman road. The track gently drops for miles — what a wonderful reward after the climb up!

As we approach the northern edge of Salisbury, I am anticipating a great view of Old Sarum. I am disappointed. Instead, the best views are to be seen behind us as we climb the gentle slope away from this spectacular hill fort. Cycling away from Salisbury without having seen the city, I ponder whether we should have allowed extra time to explore a bit more, rather than simply focusing on the journey.

For the next few miles, I keep my eyes peeled for a view of Stonehenge. I have seen it many times before, but am disappointed that I fail in my quest today.

Time is pressing, so when we realise that we have missed seeing it, we don't turn back. The landscape has now changed. Pretty villages have been replaced by homogeneous army camps, and delightful valleys by the hulk of Salisbury Plain. We pass signs indicating that the firing ranges are in use and that the road is closed.

'I think the bit we need to cycle on is still open,' I say, not totally sure.

'What do you mean, think? We can't risk cycling over the ranges when they're firing.'

Highly alert, we cycle on, looking and listening for any life-threatening activity. The further we cycle, the less sure we are of our safety. Another red flag alongside the path dissolves our resolve. We dive off-route down to the safety of a village.

By now, dusk is threatening, and we still have a few miles to cover. We stand at a junction with an A-road, discussing our options. It would be faster to ride down the road to our accommodation. On the other hand, the off-road route is enticingly quiet and looks infinitely more interesting. We choose the slower route. Bad choice! It is horribly rutted and difficult to cycle along safely. I am flagging now, struggling to concentrate.

When we accidentally miss a turning and pop back out onto the A-road, we decide that enough is enough and slip onto the road for the final part of the day's journey.

'We're almost there!' Alison calls from in front of me, as we pass a sign to the Lavingtons. I am completely exhausted, digging deep into my reserves of physical energy and mental resolve with every rotation of the pedals. It is another mile before we reach West Lavington. The village seems to just go on and on, but that is nothing compared to Market Lavington, where we are staying. We reach the village sign running on fumes and desperate to get off our bikes.

'Julia, you've got this.' I repeat my mantra, again and again.

'How long *is* this village?' I ask Alison. Not that she knows the answer; it was just my turn to whinge. 'It must be the longest village in the country!'

When we finally reach the pub, relief floods through me. Today's torture is over, and we have just arrived before it is too dark to cycle without lights.

'How far does the book say we've cycled?' Ali asks as we collapse onto our beds.

'45 miles.'

'Well, my GPS says 52.'

No wonder we're so tired!

King Alfred's Way: Market Lavington to Sparsholt (Wantage)

'Oh no, not already...'

I fumble the alarm off and pull the duvet over my head. I am not ready to start another day.

Eventually, it is the lure of breakfast that pulls me from the comfort of my bed.

A Lycra-clad cyclist greets us. 'Morning! Rules five and nine are being invoked today.' He explains that *The Rules* are maintained by the Velominati. Rule number five is to harden up, although not quite that polite. Rule number nine states that if you are out in bad weather, you are a badass. Period. The forecast is for rain all day, and it has already started. 'If you are cycling today, it's official — you are badasses!' Well, 'badass' certainly sounds better to me than 'drowned rat'!

Before leaving, we pull on waterproof jackets and cover our rucksacks. Our faces are a picture of grim determination; we are not delighting in the thought of today's cycling. Market Lavington is below Salisbury Plain and the route is on top, so the first five hundred metres of the day will be punishing, too.

As I gasp my way up the hill, Ali disappears off into the distance. I stop, catch my breath, start again — a familiar pattern by now. By the time I reach the top, steam is rising out of my jacket and I am about to explode with the heat I have generated. That's it — no more waterproof jacket for me!

We have risen from drizzle into cloud. The views to the north are purportedly excellent, but alas, non-existent for us.

My bike is a hardtail (no rear suspension), and Ali's has suspension. On rough downhill sections, I am glad of the extra stability. But on this recently laid stony track, I suffer, while Ali glides along as though she's on a croquet pitch. I am looking forward to turning off this painful path in the cloud. When we do, I am reminded of the warning to be careful what you wish for!

The track down to the village of Chilton is way beyond my capability as a rider. It is deeply rutted and chalky, so exceptionally slick when wet, as it is now. The clay surrounding the chalk flies up in clumps and cakes everything, including my face, as I try to control my slipping tyres. My heart is in my mouth all the way down, adrenaline flowing through my veins. I take a deep breath as I arrive safely at the bottom.

'Alison, I can hear a grinding noise as I cycle. Can you hear it?'

'No,' she replied, 'you're imagining it.'

A few hundred metres further along, we are on a smoother track. 'I can still hear it — let's swap bikes for a while so you know what I'm talking about.'

'Oh yes, I can hear it now. Your gears aren't indexing properly. I'll call Bob.' Thank goodness we have technical support! I describe the issue and he agrees with Ali's diagnosis. He sounds dubious as we speak.

'I can explain the fix to you, but if you get it wrong, you could completely mess things up.'

I try to persuade Alison to do the fix for me, but she doesn't want to take responsibility either — we're both cowards!

I follow Bob's instructions as closely as I can. No change.

'Did you count, like he said you should?'

'Well, sort of. It was hard to concentrate on counting, turning the knob and cycling at the same time.'

'You numpty! Counting is crucial or you could break the gears.'

I try again. Now the gears will not engage at all. I envision Bob having to come out and rescue us. I don't want to have to tell him that I have broken the bike he has taken the trouble to build for me. 'OK Julia, you've got this.' One more attempt, and it improves. A few minutes later, there is no grinding at all. I have averted disaster — with Bob's help, of course.

It is so good to be cycling on roads again — my nerves need some time to settle. But Alison is not happy.

'This ride is really sloggy.' I agree, but hearing it doesn't help.

'I'll complete the five days, but I won't do anything like this again.'

I realise that tomorrow night, we will be staying at Alison's house. I think about how hard it will be to set off again the next morning. The temptation to duck out worms its way into my head. Why should I make my friend miserable doing something that she clearly hates? And do I really want to carry on on my own?

I am looking forward to having lunch in Avebury, enjoying a cup of tea and a sandwich in the courtyard between the barns and maybe pushing the bikes through the standing stones. After a tough morning, my spirits lift as we cycle into the village. We duck left into the courtyard, avoiding the people who are milling around, all looking rather lost. It appears that they, too, expected the café to be open. Heads bowed, we push our bikes along the road to the village shop. We perch on the wall between the shop and a car park while eating our pre-packed sandwiches and drinking insipid tea from a machine. Lunch might be providing fuel for our bodies, but certainly not our spirits!

A road cyclist is sharing the wall with us. He is cycling King Alfred's Way in a punishing three days (instead of our five). He is already an hour behind schedule today because he has had to repair a broken crank. Talking to him makes me realise that, although cycling is fun and you can travel faster than on foot, there is a lot that can go wrong. Not just punctures, but chains, hydraulics, brakes, cranks, gears, the list goes on.

As it leaves Avebury, the route passes through the stone circle, so I am hoping for a good view of the stones. Although we see one or two, the view is obscured by houses, fences and trees. I wish I had spent some time walking through them before leaving the village.

It is a long slog up onto the Ridgeway, and it does not improve when we are up there. The name suggests a path that follows a ridge. It is not! It is actually a series of ridges, so the route frequently dips into gaps and climbs back out. In many places, the track itself is a series of deep, narrow ruts, separated by equally narrow ridges. The ruts are tricky to stay in without hitting the edges and the ridges are tricky to stay on without slipping off one side or the other. It is hard-going.

I continue my habit of stopping partway up each hill to catch my breath before setting off again. I am pleased that I don't have to push, but beginning to get a bit disgruntled with myself. Most of the time, I am running out of grit rather than oxygen or energy. This is a mental issue, not a physical one. Alison, as usual, cycles up everything and waits for me at the top.

I spend a lot of the afternoon talking to myself. 'I have energy.' 'My legs are strong.' 'I'm a good enough cyclist to manage this.' 'You've got this.' It feels like everything is conspiring to get me down, and I'm not always winning the battle.

Generally speaking, Alison is being very patient with me, but she could compete in the whinging Olympics. I keep my thoughts to myself. 'Yes, it's sloggy. Yes, we're still in cloud. Yes, I'm keeping you from cake every time I'm slow up a hill. I know these things. I don't need reminding every five minutes!'

We arrive at the Star Inn at Sparsholt covered in mud and exhausted. I poke my head around the bar door. 'Hello, we need to check in, but you might not want us to come inside until we've hosed ourselves down.'

'Oh no, that's fine, come on in!'

'Really? Can you see how muddy I am?' I push through the door and give a twirl.

'Really, there's no need to worry — just please don't sit on the bed until you have showered!'

Five minutes later, we are in the pub garden watching the smartly dressed bartender hosing down our bikes for us. He is absolutely insistent that we do not need to get involved, despite the mud spattering everywhere. We are too tired to argue.

Once they are clean, he moves his own bike from the cellar so that ours will fit in. That is good; we don't need to worry about our bikes overnight.

The pub is smart — quite possibly too smart for us, but if the staff feel the same way, they don't let on. The food is good, the bed is comfortable, and the shower is hot and powerful. It is just what we need, although not quite enough to shake the thought of putting an end to this misery tomorrow evening.

King Alfred's Way: Sparsholt to Fleet

I wake with a start when the alarm sounds. I have slept well, but my stomach is churning. I feel sick. Is it dread of the day to come or something I ate? As we set off, I wonder how I am going to make it back onto the ridge, feeling like this. I labour up the hill even more slowly than usual.

On the top, the clouds have lifted and there are occasional bursts of sunshine, which help to improve my mood. The cycling is less demanding this morning. The ruts are smaller, and there are a lot of downhill stretches. Freewheeling down into Streatley, I find myself smiling. My stomach has settled and the gentle Thames Valley lies ahead.

Streatley is much prettier than I remember, with weathered red brick and flint houses lining the road. We cross the river into Goring and stop at a café for a cup of tea and a bite to eat. Another two groups of cyclists tackling King Alfred's Way have also chosen this spot for a rest. Each group is taking a different approach.

Two women are planning to complete the route in three days. They are wild camping, but hardly have any gear at all on their bikes. Comfort is clearly not a priority.

The other group is travelling more sedately. There are eight of them, aiming to complete the route in the same time as us — five days. This morning, it took them two hours to regain the route. First one puncture, then another and another appeared after they accidentally cycled over some hedge trimmings. Five of their tyres had multiple punctures. Thank goodness for tubeless technology!

'Are you cycling King Alfred's Way?' We turned to see a man sitting next to the window. It is an innocent enough opening gambit, so we politely respond. He takes it as a signal to open the floodgates. Until we leave, we are deluged with his opinions on bike choices ('Ooh, are they Lauf forks?'), different methods of carrying luggage, his Sea-to-Sea trip and cycling in the Alps. Rarely for us, we can't get a word in edgeways!

From Goring to Reading, the Thames flows downhill and the cycle route follows. Although it does not hug the river, it is easy cycling. However, our rhythm is disrupted as we constantly have to stop to navigate now we are off the Ridgeway.

I smell and hear Reading before I see it. The route loops around this busy town to avoid dangerous roads. We ignore the first loop and cycle through the traffic — it is heavy but not fast, so doesn't feel too risky. The next loop seems more sensible to follow because the alternative is a fast, multi-lane A-road. As we cycle these extra miles through dull urban fringe, I cannot see any merit in the loop except for avoiding the main road, especially as heavy lorries thunder past us on the 'country' road. Where the loop re-joins the A-road, we see a cycle path that runs directly towards the town centre. It would have been safer and shorter to stick to the A-road.

Our language is blue as we join the cycle path and head south.

From this point forward, I look more closely at the route ahead and question some of the loops. Some are clearly there for a reason, others seem to have simply been created to add miles to the route rather than interest.

It is a relief to escape the bustle and fumes of Reading and re-emerge into the rolling Berkshire countryside. I wonder where and when we will find some lunch, as we haven't seen anywhere selling food since the café in Goring.

'Julia, look — bacon butties!' Ali points to a sign tied to a tree. 'It says there's a pop-up café just a 10-minute cycle away.'

Our feet speed up as our minds fly ahead.

Fifteen minutes later, Ali stops and turns.

'We must have missed it...' Our feet are slower now, and our hearts are heavier. We pedal on.

This time, it's me that spots the sign. 'Look, Ali, another sign! It says to keep on going.' We speed up again now we have the target back in our sights. If only we knew where it was! Another sign: Almost there! We keep our eyes peeled. Are we looking for a horsebox? A car with a coffee machine in the back? A converted bus? No, a house! We come to a halt by a small wooden gate leading to a large house. A middle-aged woman strides towards us.

'Bring your bikes round to the back. What would you like?'

'When I'm at home, I put the sign out and just make whatever people want. When I'm out, I put the sign away.' I'm so glad that she is open for business this afternoon!

We lounge on her lawn, relaxing as we wait for our food. I try to take a selfie with her cute dog, but he sees this as an invitation to lick my face. Dog kisses - yuck! But it was worth it — we both set off for the last part of the day's cycling feeling revitalised.

Today, I have remembered how much I enjoy cycling. The miles have been passing under my tyres almost effortlessly and I have been able to look around and appreciate the scenery.

Ali, however, hates it. She has been moaning all day. Every time we stop, she tells me how she isn't enjoying the cycling. I am convinced that she is totally miserable and wants to stop.

This evening, we are due to stay at her house, so I resolve to wait until we are there to talk to her about it. Then, I will suggest that she stays at home. I can either continue on my own or we can do something else together for the rest of the week. In reality, I am finding the ride hard, and being reminded every few minutes about how much of a slog it is makes things worse.

At Hartley Wintney, we stop to decide where to end for the day. For some reason, I can't hold it in any longer.

'Ali, I think we should cycle back to yours now. And when we get there, you should stay there. There's no point in you wasting your precious leave from work being miserable.'

She turns round to look at me square-on, a quizzical expression on her face.

'Don't be silly. I'm not hating it. We started this ride together, and we'll end it together.'

There is clearly no question in her mind about finishing the route, and there is no room for debate. She turns straight back round and cycles off along the road. We are continuing.

I fight back tears. I'm so relieved that the situation is resolved. A heavy weight has lifted from my shoulders, and with a new-found enthusiasm, I follow in her wake.

King Alfred's Way:
Fleet to Liss

This morning, the sun is shining inside and out. It feels like I have won a bonus day. Only yesterday, I was unsure about whether we would be continuing, yet here we are, on our way again. At breakfast, Ali promised to stop moaning, and she has! I have even spotted her smiling once or twice already today. The whole trip has suddenly climbed a few rungs on the enjoyment ladder. If only I had said something sooner. Not only have I started to enjoy myself more, but I'm pretty sure that she has too!

My new-found sense of delight feels great, and I start to relax.

We roll gently down into a quiet valley where a sturdy wooden bridge crosses a river. I can't resist a quick peek at the wide, shallow stream of water glinting in the sun. I am expecting it to be silvery clear, with plant fronds dancing in the flow as we saw in Wiltshire. The plants are indeed dancing, but their leaves are weighed down by sediment, which is choking the whole of the stream bed.

As my mind drifts on to poor farming practices and how they impact so many of our waterways, my bike also drifts.

Bang!

My front wheel hits one of the wooden uprights and stops dead. Luckily, the bridge is solid. Less luckily, I slide forward and hit my pubis on the handlebar post.

I curse, gasp for air and grimace, hoping for some endorphins to kick in and kill the pain. The bridge and the bike are both fine, but I wonder whether I have caused some serious damage to myself.

I don't want Ali to know how much it hurts, so I laugh and try to hold a normal conversation while the pain subsides. I gently tiptoe my bike across the rest of the bridge and ease myself back into the saddle. Good! I can cycle. No broken bones.

I ride through the Surrey Hills gleefully, quietly chuckling to myself. I don't know whether it is the familiarity of the landscape laden with happy childhood memories, the sunshine or Ali's new-found positivity that is making me so happy. Dragonflies dart around us as we stop for a break at Frensham Ponds, one of our teenage hang-outs.

The ground is now sandy, slowing us down. In some places, we both have to get off and push. Yes, both of us! Even a cycling ninja like Alison can't cope with tyres sinking ankle-deep into soft sand!

The thought of cycling up the Devil's Punchbowl at Hindhead has been looming in my mind all morning. It is reputed to be one of the hardest climbs of the route. Ali and I have been powering uphill for some time before we realise that's where we are. What a result — we are already halfway up!

At this point, the climb gets technical. It is not just steep, but also covered in loose rocks about the size of a teapot. Ali pushes on ahead, wiggling her bike from side to side to find a route through, but I don't have the skill for this. I dismount and push, but only for a few metres. I am supremely proud of myself for hardly needing to push or stop all the way up. When we reach the top, I find myself grinning from ear to ear.

A huge climb like that only means one thing — a huge downhill section. I glide down the gentle tarmac slope, my grin still in place. Ali prefers the thrill of tricky steep sections that require technical skill. She is looking bored.

On Bramshott Common, Ali suddenly whoops and disappears. Rather than blindly following, I stop and consider what lies ahead. She is already a long way down the steepest slope yet. I watch her career around the bend at the bottom. The momentum carries her a long way up the next slope before she has to start pedalling again. There is no way that I can follow at that speed.

I decide, instead, to go slowly, with some modicum of control. Bad idea! It doesn't take me long to discover that if you brake on a steep sandy hill, your back tyre will try to overtake your front one. As slowly and with as little control as thick, sticky treacle running off a spoon, I drop to the ground in slow motion. The deep, soft sand breaks my fall, so I'm not hurt, although my pride has taken another beating. Luckily, Ali is still powering up the slope ahead and hasn't seen.

I quickly lift the bike up and re-assess my strategy. Going slowly is clearly not the best plan. So, I steel myself, take a deep breath and let go of my brakes.

'Stay on the bike, Julia. Stay on the bike!'

The path twists before reaching the bottom. I can feel my face contort in concentration and try not to think about what will happen if I crash at this speed.

I fly out of the turn and away, up towards Ali. Success!

Ali is waiting for me. She laughs when I tell her what happened. 'You crashed *again*? On *that* slope!'

This is not the last chance Ali has to laugh at me crashing. The best is yet to come.

I'm cycling in the lead. The ground is flat, and the path is wide enough not to have to concentrate too hard. Although there is a background roar of traffic, I am admiring my surroundings — the spiky heather contrasting with the soft silver birches, set off by warm sunshine in a clear blue sky.

Oh look, I think. There's a twig across the path. That's OK. My bike can handle that.

I cycle on. Then my brain wakes up. That's not a twig, it's a slow worm. I wouldn't want to hurt a slow worm. How can I avoid it?

Oh no, it's not a slow worm, it's an adder! If I hurt it, it'll bite Ali! What can I do? No space to cycle around it. I know! I'll bunny-hop over it.

I have no idea where that last thought came from. I have never bunny-hopped a bike in my life. But I am milliseconds away from hitting the snake. There is no time to hatch another plan. So, I lift the front wheel and jump.

'Yes! I'm in the air! I missed it!'

CRASH!

I somersault through the air. My back smashes into the ground. My legs twist awkwardly under the bike frame.

I do a quick limb-check. Nothing bent at an unhealthy angle, no blood and no significant pain — good! I look up to see Ali on the path behind me, chortling.

To be fair, I would have done exactly the same in her position. She is still smarting from how hard I laughed when we were children, and she was thrown from a pony into a gorse bush. She was unhurt, except for thousands of needle pricks - we were pulling them out for hours afterwards!

'It was a snake,' I blurt. 'I didn't want to hurt it, and I didn't want it to bite you!'

Ali controls her laughter for long enough to reassure me that I missed the snake. It was as shocked as I was to find my bike in mid-air above it and rapidly slithered off into the undergrowth, unhurt.

There is no obvious damage to the bike either. I pick myself and the bike up, rearrange both into the correct order, and continue along the track, chuckling at myself. I hope that crashing isn't going to be my new normal.

King Alfred's Way: Liss to Winchester

This morning, I tell myself that I will stay on my bike today. I am determined that my last day will not be marred by more falls. We will be cycling on hard rocky ground, so falling off will hurt far more than yesterday's tumbles.

I know to expect some challenging climbs today, so I also picture myself cycling up hills without stopping. This is definitely a matter of optimism over experience, but I figure it is worth a try.

After weeks of pushing my bike uphill, then stopping for rests but not having to push, will this be the day that I finally get the hang of hills? I will certainly have plenty of practice as we climb onto the South Downs.

As we approach them, my heart sinks. They loom above us, and they do not form a continuous ridge — we are going to have more than one big climb today.

And of course, with every big climb is a big descent. In my determination to stay on, I find myself nervous on the steep downhill sections. I am very aware that if I fall, I will probably injure myself on this terrain. So, I find myself tensing my arms and braking even more than normal. As I become aware of what I'm doing, I start a new mantra.

'Relax, Julia.'

On an early climb, my resolve to pedal all the way is tested and found wanting. At the bottom of the hill, we let a couple of men cycle ahead of us. When they start pushing, Ali just cycles past them. But for me, it is as though they have given me permission to push too. So, I do. This is such a psychological game!

As Ali and I rest and talk about hill-climbing tactics, we let the two men pass us again. We watch as they soon stop and push up the hill ahead of us. But this time, I have determination on my side — I am not going to push just because they did.

'You can do this, Julia!'

'Ali, I did it in a oner!'

Alison chuckles. 'Well done! I told you you could. You just have to believe in yourself.'

Proclaiming my success gives me a boost, so poor Ali has to suffer the same announcement at the top of every hill for the rest of the day.

There is one hill that completely defeats me, though. The climb up from Queen Elizabeth Country Park is steep, grassy and long. Very long. I don't have the heart — or lungs — to tackle it, especially when Ali stops to take a call. I get off and push as she chats on the phone, then watch in awe as she cycles all the way to the top. She simply refuses to give up!

Navigation is easy once we reach the South Downs Way national trail, as there are waymarkers at every junction. The track is mainly wide and undemanding, so I relax and admire the view. And what a view it is! The English Channel shimmers off to our left and the Sussex Downs roll away to our right, with the ridge of the South Downs marching ahead, all under a clear blue sky. It is England at its most magnificent.

Sadly, the route into Winchester itself is not quite as magnificent. As we near the city, the countryside turns into urban fringe with piles of dog poo on the path, litter in the margins and heavy traffic thundering past.

Once we reach the buildings, though, it is only a short distance to the city centre and King Alfred's statue. As we approach, I take a video and my voice cracks with emotion. We have made it! When I walked the South West Coast Path last year, there was never a time when I doubted my ability to complete it. 200 miles on a bike appears to be less challenging than 600 on foot, but there have been a couple of days when not only did I think that maybe we wouldn't finish, but also had no interest in finishing.

Ultimately, it is only because I was with Alison that I completed the circuit. She would not have contemplated defeat, despite not particularly enjoying the ride.

As usual with any challenge, after the initial elation of completing it, there is an air of anti-climax. After all, all we have to do now is wash dog poo off our tyres and drink tea while we wait for our lift home. No more challenges and no more triumphs.

For now.

Personal Reflection

Cycling King Alfred's Way was not just a long-distance bike ride. As is the case with any adventure, there were lessons I was reminded of and others that I learnt — about myself and the wider world, as well as cycling.

I learnt about how fragile my positive state of mind can be when it is constantly being eroded. I must remember that I have control over how I react to a situation.

An even bigger lesson for me is to not simply accept what people say at face value. If I had probed more deeply, I would have realised far sooner that Ali was nowhere near as miserable as she seemed. And she might have agreed to be more positive sooner. Cycling along the ruts of the Ridgeway in cloud is never going to be much fun, but it could have been much better than it was. Having a difficult conversation with someone does not have to threaten your friendship, as long as it is approached in the right way and with empathy.

Throughout my training and the ride itself, Ali constantly told me that I was a stronger cyclist than I thought. She reminded me again and again that cycling is a mind game. 'I get to the top of hills because I know I can. You just need to learn that about yourself.' And by the end of the week, I had.

On the last day's cycling, not only did Ali put up with me glorifying my achievements every time I made it to the top of a hill, but she encouraged me to. It worked! I know that giving yourself pats on the back as you progress is valuable; this experience has driven that message home.

On the bike, when I allowed myself to be confident and relax, I found that things started to go right. Looking back on this ride, I can see that I tried to force my will on the bike. It is only with hindsight that I realise that cycling should be more like dancing, bike and rider working fluidly together towards success. I think now that Ali should have gained the trail name of 'Bike Dancer' – a name that I will try to earn for myself next time.

A few weeks after returning from this trip, I realised that the same principle applies to life more broadly. I was trying to force my will on my work and my stress levels were rising. When I relaxed a bit and focused my attention on where it really mattered, I felt better and achieved more.

The other huge lesson that I was reminded of on this trip is the importance of learning from others and having a backup in place for those skills you need but don't have. Alison and Bob are both keen — and skilled — mountain bikers and Bob understands bike mechanics. There is a surprising amount that can go wrong on a bike. Not only did he build an ideal bike for me, but he was also at the end of the phone throughout the week to provide technical support.

Alison helped me enormously with cycling technique and kit. When I first started on longer rides, I suffered from excruciating pain in my neck and out along my arms. Ali told me that if I relaxed and didn't grip the handlebars so tightly, that pain would stop. And it did. She suggested that I try changing into a low gear and spinning up hills as grinding up them was not working for me. These strategies were crucial for my enjoyment and the success of the trip. Ali lent me cycling shoes with a firm base that sticks to the pedals without having to clip in — magic! And she taught me the importance of wearing cycling shorts — without knickers underneath. I did once go out for a longer ride without my padded shorts because they were in the wash, and boy, did I find out that she was right!

We have been friends for a long time and appreciated spending these precious few days together. Despite not enjoying every moment of this trip, Ali and I are already planning our next adventure together.

Your Journey

Living *Your* Cycling Dream

This book is not just about my journey. It is here to help you achieve your own bikepacking challenges.

In *Live Your Bucket List*, I detail a process to follow to make your bucket list dreams come true. One important part of the process is to learn from others — there is no need to reinvent the wheel. The following chapters give you a chance to learn from my mistakes and triumphs to make your trip the best possible success.

It all starts with igniting your passion for your plans.

Ignite Your Dream

Cycling King Alfred's Way is hard work. It takes effort and a degree of skill. You will need to be fit and prepared for discomfort and setbacks.

The process described in *Live Your Bucket List* will help you overcome obstacles in the way of achieving your dreams. Here, I have summarised some of the key points relevant to this specific challenge. You can listen to the full Ignite Your Dream milestone of *Live Your Bucket List*, free of charge, at www.juliags.com/members.

- The first stage is to decide exactly what you are planning:
- When do you want to cycle King Alfred's Way (or another route)? Does that give you enough time to prepare, including training?
- What kind of bike will you use? A road bike is unlikely to be a good idea on King Alfred's Way. I was glad to be riding a mountain bike, but lots of people use gravel bikes too.

- How many days would you like to spend cycling? We took four and a half, and we saw others who were doing it in as little as three. If you want to enjoy the historic landscapes and visit monuments like Stonehenge along the way, you will need to allow additional time. If you are a road cyclist, your average speed will drop considerably when cycling off-road.

- What accommodation will you use? We chose to stay in B&B's. If you choose to wild camp or bivvy, you will carry more weight but might not need to cycle off the route every night to reach your accommodation.

- Will you carry your luggage or use a baggage-carrying company?

- Are you going to cycle alone, with a friend or in a group?

If this ride will be a challenge for you, then you might want to think about how to overcome any potential stumbling blocks.

- What are your reasons for not having cycled this route already? These might include things like lack of fitness, not having the right type of bike, not having someone to go with, needing to save up, or struggling to find the time.

- Are there any other reasons you can think of why you might find yourself shying away from the challenge now? What limiting beliefs do you have that might stop you, e.g. too old, too young, not good enough, can't afford it? What do you fear if you pursue this dream?

- For each of these potential stumbling blocks, what can you do to smash them or sidestep them?

The final step to take to fully ignite your dream is to understand more about your 'why'.

- Consider all the reasons you have for wanting to cycle the route, and the strength of each.
- Then, consider all the reasons you have for NOT wanting to cycle it, and the strength of each of those.
- Do the positives outweigh the negatives? If not, is there anything you can do to strengthen the positives or reduce the significance of the negatives?

That's the logical element of decision-making covered, but to make a decision that sticks, you need to be emotionally engaged, too.

- How will you feel once you have achieved your dream? Picture yourself at the end of the challenge. Who or what will you be grateful for? What skills have you developed? What challenges will you have overcome?
- And how will you feel if you don't pursue your dream? Imagine how you will feel in a year, five years and ten years. How does this compare to being committed to achieving your dream?

If you're not that bothered, then this exercise should help you realise that, and you can focus on a different dream.

Conversely, if you are now excited, if this is something that you really want to do, then it's time to book your accommodation, agree on dates with your cycling buddies and start planning your trip.

Make a Plan

If you break the challenge down into stages, it makes the planning easier. In broad terms, your plan will need to include:

- Finding the resources you need, including your bike, clothing and luggage system. For the latter, we used small backpacks with hydration bladders and took as little else as we thought we could get away with.

- Training. How long do you think you will need to get fit enough? What sort of cycling will you need to do? I was fairly walking-fit already and gave myself 6 weeks to get cycle-fit. During this period, I did some sprints (cycling as far as I could in an hour), some longer days to build up my cycling stamina, and spent some more technically demanding time on the Malvern Hills.

- Booking accommodation.

- Booking time for the ride itself.

- Time to reflect and recover. Will you want to go back to work the next day, or allow yourself some recovery time?

One of the key elements of planning is to learn from other people who have completed the same, or a similar, challenge. I learnt a lot from my cycling buddy Alison and her partner, Bob. You are already taking a step towards this by learning from my experience.

- Who do you know who could help you prepare for the challenge?

Here are some useful places to find out more about cycling King Alfred's Way:

- Cycling UK's website. You can download the GPX files there, and order a copy of the guidebook. The guidebook gives information on the historical context of the landscape, practical tips on how to manage the route, OS maps, descriptions of the route and suggested itineraries.
- Cycling UK's Facebook page for all things King Alfred's Way.
- Guy Kesteven, the author of Cycling UK's guidebook, has produced some videos of himself cycling the route. Head over to YouTube to find them.

Some key recommendations from me, a novice bikepacker. As with any advice, take what you find useful and ignore anything that won't work for you:

- Take a navigation system with clear directional arrows that you can read as you cycle. Whenever we were off the National Trails (most of the route), our ride did not flow well because we were forever stopping to check where we were and which direction we should head in next.

- Consider a tubeless tyre system. One thing we did not have to worry about was punctures.
- Wear padded shorts!
- Train on the sort of terrain you will be riding on. For King Alfred's Way, this includes narrow ruts; knobbly, gnarly slopes; loose ground; and steep sections of hill, both up and down.
- Relax. When you tense up, your bike will effectively also tense and stop moving as well as it should.
- Take front and rear lamps just in case you end up cycling in poor visibility.

You will need to think about what might go wrong on your trip and prepare for it as far as is sensible.

- Do you know how to deal with routine problems like punctures?
- Do you need to learn about bike maintenance for less routine issues, or do you have someone who could provide support, as we did?
- What will you do if your phone runs out of power and you are using it to navigate, or need it to call the emergency services? We carried additional battery packs, a whistle (give six sharp blows if you need help in the UK, three around the rest of the world) and the guidebook containing a paper map.
- Do you know what to do if you or one of your cycling companions is injured? I have basic first aid knowledge and we took a small first aid kit with us that focused on broken bones (a bandage), grazes (large wound dress-

ings), a tick remover, and, not strictly first aid, ibuprofen in case of painful joints. We also took Sudocrem to treat any chafing. What will you want to include in yours?

- What other contingency situations do you foresee?

As part of your planning, take a moment to think about your strengths and how they could help you. They might have nothing to do with cycling, but still be useful. For example, if you are a good baker, then you might make some healthy energy bars to take with you or reward yourself by baking a cake if you complete your training as planned.

Also, consider your weaknesses. How can you sidestep, manage or overcome them?

The final two elements of your plan are to consider how you are going to find the time and the money to complete your dream.

- When can you fit your training in? Is there something else that you need to stop doing for a while to give you more time?
- Do you need to book time off work for the ride itself? If you can't take the time off work, could you do it in sections instead?
- How much money do you need? If you need to reduce the cost, could you buy second-hand kit? Or borrow a bike, as I did? Could you camp instead of staying in B&B's? How long will you need to save up, or can you just pay for it out of your existing savings or income?

Once all these elements are in place, it's time to get out there and implement your plan.

Implement Your Plan

Planning is an essential part of the process, but a plan means nothing until you put it into practice. It's time to get moving!

If you're lucky, everything will go smoothly, but when has that ever happened in real life?

When things get a bit bumpy, you can help yourself stay on track using a few simple techniques.

One is the power of self-talk.

- I often used mantras to get me through the hard times on the King Alfred's Way. What mantras could you adopt to help you? Try saying them out loud to yourself to give them more power.

- What negative stories do you tell yourself that might get in the way, e.g. 'I'm no good at cycling up hills?' What can you do to change these stories? There's no need to lie to yourself. Just think about how you can reframe things. Would the thought, 'I'm improving on hills,' serve you better?

When you are completing a challenge like training for and cycling a long distance, it is more important than ever to look after yourself. During the ride itself, Ali and I put electrolytic tablets in our water to help reduce muscle stiffness, and they seemed to work. When I backpacked the South West Coast Path over a period of weeks, I became severely deficient in iron. This is something that endurance athletes, and women in particular, can suffer from, so now I take iron supplements when I'm training hard.

- What do you need to do to look after your health while you are training and cycling the route itself?
- Do you need to eat particularly healthily or take supplements?
- I struggled during the first three days of the ride because Alison was moaning so much. She stopped as soon as she realised what an impact it was having on me. Do you need to ask someone to be more positive or supportive? Do you need to avoid anyone while you are completing this challenge to protect your positive state of mind?
- Is your training likely to affect other areas of your life? Is there any way you can mitigate the effect?

Sometimes, an unforeseen event will threaten to knock you off course. If that happens, try reviewing your reason for deciding to go bikepacking. Then consider your options:

- Do you need to shift your attention to deal with this unforeseen event and park your dream of bikepacking for now?

- Is it possible to adapt your plans, e.g. cycling the route in sections rather than as a whole?
- Are there any new advantages to gain from this unforeseen event?
- Can you still do something towards the challenge? If not, is it time to consider tackling another bucket list dream while you are unable to pursue this one?

If you want to make the most of your experience, read on for one final stage of the process.

The End of the Road –
Celebrate & Reflect

Congratulations on completing your challenge! How do you feel — excited? Satisfied? A bit deflated? At the end of any journey you have been focusing on for a while, it is natural to feel a sense of disappointment that it has come to an end, as well as excitement that you have achieved your goal.

It is tempting to start to plan your next adventure immediately, and that is just what Alison and I did.

But before putting this journey to bed, there is one more step to complete, and that is celebration and reflection.

When Ali and I completed King Alfred's Way, we went for a blow-out Chinese meal with Bob to celebrate our achievement. This was a real treat for me and a great way to celebrate.

- How are you going to mark your achievement?

Writing this book has helped me to consolidate my memories of the trip. Next, I will sort through my photos and videos and create a slideshow for myself that I can look back on and enjoy.

- How will you consolidate your memories?

This is also a good time to reflect on your journey. One of my greatest lessons from this experience is to probe more and not just accept what people are saying to me, especially when it is having a significant impact on how I'm feeling. I have also learnt to have more confidence in my ability, relax and let things happen rather than trying to force them.

- What skills have you developed?
- What have you learnt about yourself? And others?
- How have you changed?
- How can you apply this learning to your everyday life?

Bonus Chapter
Ali's Response

Having written so much about my friend and cycling buddy Ali, I thought it only fair that she should have a chance to respond and tell something of her experience.

Did you really moan as much as Julia makes out?

Unfortunately, the answer has to be yes! I think Julia and I set out with different mindsets when we undertook this trip. For Julia, it was about the views, sights and the experience. I have done biking trips before, including journey trips, but these were all off-road and very technical in lots of places. My mission on this ride was to get from start to finish each day as quickly as possible with as few stops as possible, ideally with cake!

We chose this route as it was sold as an off-road trip. I mainly do technical mountain biking and don't like road riding. As Julia hadn't done much biking before, King Alfred's Way sounded like a good compromise for us to cycle together. Unfortunately, a lot of the first couple of days were on the road. This meant I wasn't in my happy place. Hence, lots of moaning.

Did you feel better after you told Julia that you were going to stop moaning, or did she imagine it?

Although I knew I was complaining, it was only once we hit the low point of Julia suggesting I stay at home that I realised how my attitude was affecting her. I gave myself a good talking to. I realised that my attitude had been wrong all along. Even in your 50s, you can learn about yourself! This realisation had an immediate effect, and I then enjoyed the rest of the trip. It helped that the sun came out, and the trip became more off-road and wooded. Riding dirt tracks in the sunshine is my idea of a perfect day on the bike. However, the main factor in the improvement of my mood was realising how moaning had been making both of us feel. It was making us both miserable. Once I stopped, we both felt great.

Did Julia moan a lot, too?

I would love to say yes, but no, she didn't. I found the riding much easier than Julia. Despite this, whenever she struggled up the hills, she just persisted until she got to the top. Part of her hill issue was her mindset and part was technique. At the beginning, I don't think Julia believed she could get up the hills in one go. Once she believed in herself more, she got up them much better. Julia has always been driven. If she decides to do something, she will – this is what happened with the hills.

What advice would you give about cycling King Alfred's Way?

Lots of people have undertaken this trip and really enjoyed it. For me, it seems like more of a road rider or cross-country rider's trip, or for someone who enjoys a ride even when it gets sloggy. I would do the last part again as I enjoyed the riding, but the rest of it wasn't for me.

My advice would be to make sure that someone in your group knows how to map-read. It is Julia's map-reading that got us from start to finish each day. If the navigation had been left to me, we'd still be cycling!

What advice would you give about travelling with old friends?

Julia and I have done a couple of trips together recently. I joined her on the South West Coast Path and didn't moan. I would advise that you speak up if you are unhappy with a situation, and hopefully it will get resolved as it did in our case.

Final words

Julia and I have been friends for about 47 years – this is scary but true. We have been in and out of each other's lives to a greater or lesser extent as we have grown up and as life changes, but we have always been friends. What I find interesting is the fact that we are so different but still get along really well. I don't like change. I have had different jobs but still live near where we grew up. Julia is the opposite – she thrives on change. She has moved all over the country and had a wide variety of jobs. If she tells me she's going to do something, I believe it, even if it's strange or extreme, and she generally does it. We have opposing views on lots of things, but despite all this, we have a great friendship.

An Invitation

Congratulations on reaching the end of this journey! What are you going to do next?

Whatever it is, if you have found this book useful, then you will love *Live Your Bucket List*, which guides you through this process in more detail. It will support you through your journey to achieve any of your bucket list dreams, from deciding which to pursue first; igniting your passion for that dream; overcoming obstacles such as fear, lack of money and time; planning to achieve your dream; implementing your plans; and reflecting on your journey. You can pick it up wherever you usually buy books from or listen to the audiobook on all the normal channels.

You can listen to the introduction and first three chapters of *Live Your Bucket List*, free of charge, at www.juliags.com/members.

I always appreciate receiving feedback so I can make the next version of this and future books better. I love hearing what you have to say — please leave me an honest review or email me.

And if you are looking for an inspiring and entertaining speaker for a meeting, event or broadcast, please give me a shout.

julia@juliags.com

www.juliags.com

@juliagsadventure

@juliagsadventure

Julia Goodfellow-Smith

Acknowledgements

First and foremost, I would like to thank Ali & Bob for their roles in this adventure. I am honoured to be able to call them friends.

I would also like to thank everyone else who helped me along the way: The Towpath Angels for repairing the broken chain; Dirt Works bike shop in West Malvern for releasing the clamped brakes without breaking anything; Neil Adamson for acting as chauffeur; the bartender at the Star Inn for hosing down our bikes; and the other cyclists we met and chatted to en route.

Then, there are the people who have helped me produce the book. Thank you to Mike for giving your critical views of the manuscript; Jon Doolan, my editor, for helping me knock the book into shape; Alejandro Martin for excellent cover design and formatting; everyone in the Facebook community who helped me choose a title, cover design and blurb, especially Paul Cussins for the title idea; and Fern Chan, for sharing your knowledge and immutable energy with me during our accountability calls.

Last, but by no means least, I would like to thank the launch team for everything you have done to make this book a success.

About the Author

Julia Goodfellow-Smith is an ordinary person who is doing something extraordinary — living her bucket list.

Although she was not a cyclist, as soon as she heard about Cycling UK's King Alfred's Way route, she added it to her bucket list. It didn't take long before she was cycling the path with her friend Alison. She would like to help others do the same, which is why she has written this book.

Julia has held a variety of management and consultancy roles in a range of sectors including conservation volunteering, banking and construction. She is currently focusing her attention on adventure, writing and presenting.

Julia lives in Wales with her husband Mike, and loves their daily walks along the beach. She is a member of Rotary International and Toastmasters International, a Fellow of the Royal Society of Arts and a Senator of Junior Chamber International (JCI).

Lightning Source UK Ltd.
Milton Keynes UK
UKHW012226250822
407777UK00003B/937

9 780863 194832